IT'S ALL ABOUT...

KU-577-275

FAST
CARS

KINGFISHER

First published 2016 by Kingfisher
This edition published in 2021 by Kingfisher
an imprint of Macmillan Children's Books
The Smithson, 6 Briset Street, London, EC1M 5NR
Associated companies throughout the world
www.panmacmillan.com

Series editor: Sarah Snashall
Series design: Little Red Ant and Laura Hall
Adapted from an original text by Chris Oxlade and Thea Feldman

ISBN 978-0-7534-4639-3

Copyright © Macmillan Publishers International Ltd 2016, 2021

9 8 7 6 5 4 3 2 1
1TR/0121/WKT/UG/128MA

EU representative: Macmillan Publishers Ireland Limited,
Mallard Lodge, Lansdowne Village, Dublin 4

A CIP catalogue record for this book is available from the British Library.

Printed in China

Picture credits
The Publisher would like to thank the following for permission to reproduce their material.
Top = t; Bottom = b; Centre = c; Left = l; Right = r
Front cover, p1 Shutterstock/Rodrigo Garrido; Back cover Shutterstock/Richard Thornton;
Pages 2–3, 10–11, 30–31 Shutterstock/Max Earey; 4–5 Shutterstock/jiawangkun; 5t Getty/
Donaldon Collection; 5b Alamy/PC Jones; 6 Franz Haag; 7 Alamy/JELLE vanderwolf;
8–9 Alamy/culture-images GmbH; 9t Alamy/Heritage Image Partnership Ltd; 9b Alamy/
focusonmycar.com; 11t Alamy/Peter Wheeler; 11b Alamy/WENN Ltd; 12–13 Shutterstock/
EvrenKalinBack; 13 Shutterstock/Action Sports Photography; 14 Shutterstock/Ahmad Faizal
Yahya; 15t, 32 Shutterstock/David Acosta Allely; 15b Shutterstock/efcreata mediagroup;
16–17 Shutterstock/Alexander Kosarev; 17t Shutterstock/Christian Vinces; 18 Getty/David
Madison; 19 Getty/David Taylor; 20–21 Shutterstock/Peter Weber; 21 Shutterstock/Action
Sports Photography; 22–23 Alamy/Pictorial Press; 23t Getty/Handout; 23b Alamy/AF Archive;
24 Shutterstock/vladimir salman; 25 Corbis/Tim Wright; 26 Shutterstock/charnsitr; 27t NASA
27b Shutterstock/Mike Flippo; 28 AeroMobil; 29t Shutterstock/Joseph Sohm; 29b Alamy/
SiliconValleyStock.

Front cover: A Citroen DS3 races in the 2013 Acropolis Rally of Greece.

CONTENTS

For your free audio download go to

http://panmacmillan.com/FastCars
or goo.gl/OwJXQu

Happy listening!

Scan me!

Cars all around   **4**

The first cars   **6**

Built for speed   **8**

Supercars   **10**

Track racers   **12**

Formula One   **14**

Rally racing   **16**

The fastest car   **18**

Custom cars   **20**

Movie cars   **22**

In the factory   **24**

Electric cars   **26**

Cars of the future   **28**

Glossary   **30**

Index   **32**

Cars all around

Cars come in many shapes and sizes. There are tiny cars and long cars. There are electric cars and bulletproof cars. And, of course, there are fast cars.

SPOTLIGHT: Ford Thunderbird

Manufacturer:	Ford Motor Company
Famous for:	first 'personal luxury car'
First built:	1955
Top speed:	193 km/h (120 mph)

FACT...

The American Dream is the longest car in the world. It is 30.5 metres long and has a helipad.

The tiny Peel Trident is just 183 centimetres long and 99 centimetres wide.

The first cars

Early cars looked a bit like horse-drawn carriages. They had big wheels and tiny engines, and they were very slow.

The Flocken Elektrowagen was the first electric car.

When cars were invented, most roads were rough tracks. There were no petrol stations, so drivers took cans of petrol with them in their car. Drivers also had to know how to mend their own car.

FACT...

When the first cars started driving on the roads, a man with a red flag walked in front to warn slow-moving horse-drawn carriages.

Built for speed

Sports cars are built for speed. They have a smooth, rounded shape, a powerful engine and wide tyres that grip the road as they race around corners. Sports cars are exciting to drive, although they don't have room for lots of passengers and luggage.

The Lotus Elise can travel at speeds of up to 240 kilometres per hour (150 mph).

The Prince Henry
Austro-Daimler was
one of the first
sports cars.

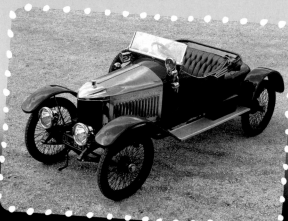

The Mazda MX-5
is one of the
bestselling sports
cars in the world.

Supercars

Supercars are the fastest, rarest and most expensive sports cars. They have an incredibly powerful engine and a very lightweight body. Only a few of each model are made, and each car can cost over one million pounds.

Bugatti Veyron Supersport: top speed 431 km/h (268 mph)

FACT...

Supercars can drive at more than 400 kilometres per hour (250 mph). That's as fast as a speeding express train.

Spotlight: McLaren F1

Manufacturer: McLaren Automotive
Famous for: fastest production car in its day
First built: 1992
Top speed: 391 km/h (243 mph)

Hennessey Venom GT:
top speed 435 km/h (270 mph)

Track racers

You can see the thrills and spills of car racing at a race track. There are races for sports cars and for special racing cars. There are even races for family cars.

Road cars race around a track in Istanbul, Turkey.

The drivers sit inside a strong cage that protects them in case they crash. They wear a fireproof suit and a helmet.

FACT...

Racing drivers usually stop in the pits during a race to change the car's tyres. Their team can change all four tyres in just eight seconds.

All four tyres are usually changed at the same time during a pit stop.

Formula One

The fastest race cars are Formula One cars. They are specially built for track racing, with top-quality tyres and a low body to grip the surface of the track.

Formula One cars race in a series of races called Grand Prixes. At the end of the season there are two champions: one driver and one car constructor.

In a Formula One race, cars can reach speeds of 320 km/h (200 mph) or more.

SPOTLIGHT: Mercedes F1 W05

Manufacturer:	Mercedes
Famous for:	Constructor Champion 2014
First built:	2014
Top speed:	estimated 300 km/h (186 mph)

Formula One driver Jenson Button prepares to race.

Rally racing

Rally races do not take place on a race circuit. Instead, the cars race from one point to another travelling along muddy roads and dirt tracks, choosing their own route. Sometimes they race through the snow and over frozen lakes.

Some rally races go across the desert.

FACT ...

In the Dakar Rally, one of the world's longest rally races, cars can drive for up to 900 kilometres each day across sand dunes, rocks, grass and mud.

The fastest car

The current land speed record is held by Thrust SSC, a jet-propelled, supersonic car. In 1997, fighter pilot Andy Green drove Thrust SSC at 1228 kilometres per hour (763 mph) in the desert in Nevada, USA.

New cars that might break the land speed record in the future are the Bloodhound SSC and the North American Eagle.

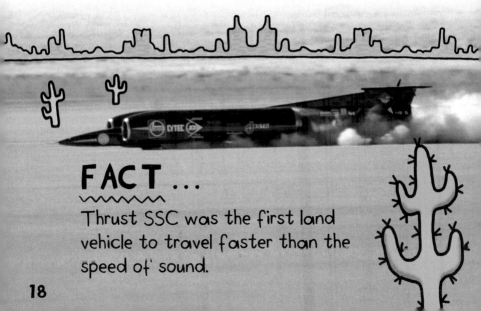

FACT...

Thrust SSC was the first land vehicle to travel faster than the speed of sound.

Thrust SSC travels faster than some jet planes.

SPOTLIGHT: Thrust SSC

Manufacturer:	SSC Programme Limited
Famous for:	holds world land speed record
First built:	1996
Top speed:	1228 km/h (763 mph)

Custom cars

Some car owners make their cars look weird and wonderful. They take off parts and add new ones, such as mirrors and wheels. Sometimes owners even change the actual shape of the car.

FACT...

Drag racers use parachutes to
slow down at the end of a race.

Some custom cars are built for
drag racing. These are
called dragsters.
They race each
other along a short
track at high speed.

Custom cars are often painted
with amazing patterns and
colourful pictures.

21

Movie cars

The most exciting cars sadly don't exist at all – except in films. James Bond's car, the Batmobile and Chitty Chitty Bang Bang all have impossible extra features. When writers create these cars they can let their imagination fly.

James Bond drives an Aston Martin equipped with rockets and an ejector seat.

FACT ...

In the 2006 film *Cars*, all the characters are... cars!

The Batmobile has sophisticated weapons and special shields.

In the factory

Most cars are made in huge factories. Machines press and fold sheets of metal to make the car's body.

Robots do most of the work in a car-building factory.

FACT...

Car makers build more than 50 million new cars every year. That's one and a half cars every second!

The body moves through the factory. As it moves, the engine, the seats, the doors and all the other parts are fixed onto it. When the car is finished, it is tested to make sure all the parts work properly.

Cars containing crash-test dummies are crashed at high speed to check how safe they are.

Electric cars

Most of the 1000 million cars in the world run on petrol or diesel. They pollute Earth's atmosphere.

Electric cars run off a huge battery. They are quiet and do not pollute the air, but they can't travel very far before they need to be recharged.

A hybrid car has both an engine and an electric motor. They use much less fuel than normal cars but are very expensive.

It can take about eight hours to recharge an electric car.

Cars of the future

What kinds of car will we be driving in the future? Believe it or not, flying cars and driverless cars have already been developed. Flying cars have wings that can be tucked away. Driverless cars use cameras and sensors to drive.

AeroMobil's flying car has an autopilot and two parachutes.

The solar cells on this car use energy from sunlight to make electricity for the engine.

Google's driverless car uses a very detailed map to find its way around.

FACT ...

It takes three minutes for AeroMobil's flying car to transform from a car into a plane.

GLOSSARY

atmosphere The layer of gases around Earth (or around any planet).

constructor A person or company that builds something.

crash-test dummy A life-sized doll used to see what might happen to people in a car accident.

custom car A car that is one of a kind because it has been built to order or has been changed in some way.

diesel A type of fuel used in some cars.

engine The part of a car that makes it move.

fuel A liquid that burns inside an engine.

hybrid car A car that uses both electricity and fuel to run.

jet-propelled Something that is moved along by a jet engine.

land speed record The record for any vehicle travelling along the ground.

motor A machine that spins to provide movement. An electric motor changes electricity into movement energy.

parachute A large piece of cloth joined to thin ropes. It slows down dragster cars and people who are falling from a plane.

pits A special area at a race track where cars stop to have their wheels changed and fuel topped up.

pollution Waste that humans put into the environment. Gases from car engines are one kind of pollution.

production car A car that is mass produced in a factory for general use on the road.

rally A long-distance car race that often passes through places where it is difficult to drive.

recharge To refill a battery with electricity when the battery has run down.

INDEX

Batmobile 22
batteries 26
Benz, Karl 7
Bond, James 22
Bugatti Veyron 10

car factories 24–25
Chitty Chitty Bang
  Bang 22
custom cars 20–21

diesel 26, 30
drag racing 21
dragsters 21
driverless cars 28, 29

electric cars 4, 6, 26,
  27, 29
engines 6, 8, 10, 25,
  27, 29

flying cars 28, 29
Formula One 14–15
fuel 27

Grand Prixes 14

hybrid cars 27
Lotus Elise 8

Mazda MX-5 9
McLaren F1 11
Mercedes F1 15

petrol 7, 26
pollution 26

racing 12–13, 14–15,
  16–17, 21
racing drivers 13
rallies 16–17
rally cars 16–17

speed records 18–19
sports cars 8–9
supercars 10–11

Thrust SSC 18, 19
tyres 8, 13, 14